U CAN'T TOUCH THIS !
M.C. HAMMER OFFICIAL PHOTO ALBUM

U CAN'T TOUCH THIS !
M.C. HAMMER OFFICIAL PHOTO ALBUM
Text by Bruce Dessau

BOXTREE

First published in the UK 1991

by BOXTREE LIMITED, 36 Tavistock Street, London WC2E 7PB
By arrangement with Winterland Productions

 © 1991 WINTERLAND PRODUCTIONS ROCK EXPRESS ®

Copyright: © 1991 Bustin' Productions, Inc.

Text: Bruce Dessau

All rights reserved

ISBN 1 8 5283 685 7

12345678910

Principle Photography: George Livingston
Additional Photography: Kerry Brown, Serge Thomann, Tony Mott
Designed and edited by Blackjacks

Flag artwork: Dave Bull

Merchandise photography: Paul Forrester

Front cover design: Paterson Jones

Printed in England by Clays Ltd., St. Ives plc

A CIP catalogue record for this book is available from the British Library.

We toured around the world from London to the Bay and without you, the greatest fans in the world, it just wouldn't have been possible.

Growing up in East Oakland, I often dreamed of seeing the rest of the world. Television provided a glimpse of many different places, but I've always been the type of person who needs to see things for myself. I give thanks that my music has allowed me to travel and meet so many wonderful people all over the world.

The Posse and I enjoyed sharing our music and dancing with you. We heard your screams and applause. Thanks for your love and support because without you, there's no Hammer.

M. C. HAMMER

Little Hammer

Looking back it was inevitable that M.C. Hammer would be a superstar. As a child at home in Oakland, California he would sit in front of the television mesmerised whenever film of James Brown's legendary Apollo Theatre show appeared. At the time - the '60s - the Godfather Of Soul was at his peak. Even then young Stanley Kirk Burrell would try to copy him.

Back then success seemed like another world. The Burrell parents were separated and Stanley's mother, who was a secretary, needed welfare payments to bring up her seven children. Times were hard and there were no guarantees of work for the young Stanley. Though reflecting on his past, at the time things didn't seem so bad. "My childhood was only tough looking back. When I was living it, it wasn't tough at all. You don't know that you are poor until you meet somebody who is rich."

It was while at school that M.C. Hammer acquired the second part of his current name. He had always dreamt of being a baseball player, and whilst doing a James Brown impression in the Oakland A's club car park, he was spotted by Charlie Finley, the owner. Stanley asked Mr Finley if he could get him into the stadium to see the game and Finley did so. He was eventually hired as a clubhouse attendant, and it was there that somebody noticed Stanley's likeness to the great player Hammerin' Hank Aaron. At first he was known as Little Hammer, but as he grew up the Little went for obvious reasons.

It was still a few years before the M.C. - Master of Ceremonies - tag was added. In the meantime Hammer had to find a way of making some money to help support his family. Many of Hammer's friends became involved in crime. Today many of his closest neighbours are doing time in San Quentin prison. Some of the people he employs in his organisation are ex-convicts to whom Hammer has given jobs to prevent them from drifting back into a life of crime. Hammer came close to being dragged into this web of vice himself. He recalls how a few times he helped out when his friends were committing robberies. "I'd say, 'I'll tell you what, you all work it out and I'll stand about two blocks down the road and be the lookout.' But just being the lookout made me sweat. I wasn't cut out for that." At heart Hammer was honest, so he decided to go to East Los Angeles College to study communications.

College just didn't feel right. Despite having a good head for business Hammer could never visualise himself in a suit reading the news, so he left. He knew that if he didn't settle down to something he might still drift into crime, so one day he went to the nearest recruiting office and joined the Navy. It was there that the beginnings of the strict, well-disciplined, directioned young man emerged. As a child his brother Louis Burrell, now his personal manager, remembers that "We were always trying to find things to do together to earn money. The determination has always been there."

If James Brown and the Navy had played their part in pushing Hammer in the direction of music, it was God that had the biggest influence. When he came out of the Navy, Hammer became a born-again Christian. For a while he considered becoming a minister, and turned to bible study. But crucially he also turned to music. Inspired by the rapping of the Sugarhill Gang's influential single, Rapper's Delight, Hammer tried to mix rap and religion by forming a gospel group called the Holy Ghost Boys. One of their numbers was **Pray**, which in a modified form was to become one of Hammer's biggest hits.

The Holy Ghost Boys never quite made it, but they laid the foundation for Hammer's current success. After they split he recorded his first solo record, **Ring 'Em**, in his basement. Unable to get major record labels interested, he set up his own label, Bust It Records, with the financial backing of a couple of baseball players from the Oakland A's. He distributed the records himself, selling them out of the boot of his car. He first built his reputation around the Californian clubs, and then all around the country. Due to this his first album, **Feel My Power**, sold an impressive fifty thousand copies. Suddenly the music business began to sit up and take notice. Hammer signed Bust It to Capitol Records who re-released his debut as **Let's Get It Started** in 1988, which spawned three top ten singles and sold over a million copies, earning Hammer his first platinum disc...
The rest, as they say, is history.

Here Comes The Hammer

With the punctuality of a space mission, the house lights go down at 9.15pm, and the audience nearly scream the roof off in anticipation. But before the big entrance there are a few preliminaries. The music that emerges from the speakers isn't from any of M.C. Hammer's albums, it's Thus Spake Zarathustra, the symphonic anthem better known as the theme from 2001: A Space Odyssey. And the deep, chilling voice that fills the hall preparing the audience for the entrance sounds more like Freddy Krueger than M.C. Hammer as it welcomes "The man, the myth, the legend, the doctor."

For a moment the stage is bare, but not for long. Suddenly the music starts, the lights go up, the band are in position and the stage is overrun by bodies, nearly thirty, male and female, spinning, splitting, flipping and performing the kind of athletic feats that would hospitalise most of the audience if they tried to emulate them.

Then in a flash of fireworks M.C. Hammer appears, like a genie summoned magically out of his bottle and plugged into the National Grid, firing on all cylinders in a dazzling golden outfit and flying across the stage. Plumes of smoke billow up into the air, and it really is 'showtime.'

There is almost too much to take in at one sitting. Something different seems to be going on in every nook and cranny of the vast stage. There's backing vocalists Real Seduction doing a soft-shoe

shuffle on one podium. Hawaiian dancer Yo-Yo twisting herself into unbelievable gyroscopic twirls on another. The rest of the dancers are behind Hammer, with the band and mad professor DJ Bryant Marable on staggered, raised levels at the back. It's fortunate that drummer Tyrone Duncan, hidden by a huge kit and perched precariously stage right, doesn't suffer from vertigo.

bone, played by Ray Brown, Gary Bias and Reggie Young respectively. They are collectively known as The Horns of Fire because they regularly play with funk champions Earth, Wind and Fire.

The brass section flesh out the riffs to Hammer's theme as he sings **Here Comes The Hammer**, and slides across the stage like James Brown on ice.

explains how he is different and how other rappers who spend all their time bragging about themselves won't last - 'A minute or two and I'm rollin'/A whole new style that people are holding on to/I move I groove I rap/You're through you're so plain/Your ego's so big that you missed the whole train/And game my friend/The people wanted more, that's why the Hammer's in.'

The sound is fuller and more muscular than on record.

Everything is suddenly brighter, bolder and literally brassier. Where most rap artists make do with a DJ mixing records at the back, Hammer has taken rap into the mainstream of live performance. He's put together a real band, which now includes a trio of trumpet, saxophone and trom-

The audience chip in with encouraging cries of "Go Hammer Go" but it's hardly needed. Hammer switches and swaps places with his dancers, and they take it in turns to make death-defying runs across the precarious edges of the stage.

You could take the lyrics to **Here Comes The Hammer** as his manifesto. In one verse he

At the front, and already glistening with sweat, Hammer combines athletic skills with rapping. Lunging forward, hands on hips, and leaning into the audience, he announces his own arrival with a song that is proud but never boastful. Hammer never makes promises he can't keep - if there's one thing that's true about his show it is the fact that he 'makes it smooth.'

It was Hammer's devotion to dance music and tireless touring which helped to establish him with his first album, **Let's Get It Started**. But he needed to take things higher, and get to places that there simply weren't enough hours in the day to get to in person. Hammer had already reached the top again with his second album, **Please Hammer Don't Hurt 'Em**, which has already sold more than fifteen million copies worldwide and become the best selling rap album of all time. He still needed something else to make people who hadn't seen his live performances realise that he was more than just another rapper, another Bobby Brown or Tone Loc. The answer was the pop video.

Of all Hammer's rivals and peers, he has taken videos one step further, turning them into mini-movies in their own right. Having made his name with a series of video shorts which were put together as **Hammer Time**, the workaholic went on to write and star in his own hour-long film, **Please Hammer Don't Hurt 'Em**.

Hammer Time pulls together the sharpest cuts from his two albums, starting, as you would expect, with **Let's Get It Started**. In stark contrast to his live show the video is a sparse affair - there are fewer dancers and no band - but it doesn't matter when a mover like Hammer is on form. The camera sticks to Hammer like glue, catching him swooping, sliding and jiving across the floor. There's no story, but there's more than enough drama to Hammer's

M.C. Hammer with his 1990 MTV Best Dance Video award.

dancing to capture everyone's attention. As the man says himself, "I am a complete entertainer, dancing and rapping, mixed in with good vocals. In my songs it all comes together."

Turn This Mutha Out has a narrative to it. In a depression-era setting, Hammer looks more like a '30s mobster than a '90s superstar. His buddy accuses him of not being a hit in New York. He spoke too soon, as the West Coast homeboy hits Harlem with leaps and bounds, ending up with a Broadway ticker tape reception fit for a President.

They Put Me In The Mix - the song that accompanied his American advertisement for Pepsi - sees Hammer really hitting the big-time. The trousers are getting roomier, the lycra tighter and the set more extravagant. The promo is one of the few which focuses on his live show, but even here there's a twist - you see the security cops in the audience smiling and getting down to the beat.

It's without doubt the video for **U Can't Touch This** that has pushed Hammer into the '90s consciousness. From the opening thud of the bass line, the screen explodes in a riot of kaleidoscopic aerobics. Hammer stands at the front wagging his finger as his dancers shimmy and shake behind him, defying gravity. But anything his posse can do, Hammer can do better, as he spins like a dervish in the forefront. It is no surprise that this promo captured both the Best Rap Video and Best Dance Video prizes at last year's MTV Awards.

A ticket, a staff pass and a necklace from Hammer's sell-out UK tour.

M.C. HAMMER RECORD AWARDS

Australia - Platinum
Canada - Platinum x 7
Chile - Platinum
France - Gold
Germany - Gold
Holland - Gold
Hong Kong - Gold
Indonesia - Gold
Japan - Platinum x 2
South Korea - Platinum x 2
Malaysia - Platinum x 2
Mexico - Platinum x 2
New Zealand - Platinum x 3
Phillipines - Platinum x 2
Singapore - Platinum x 2
South Africa - Gold
Spain - Platinum
Switzerland - Gold
Taiwan - Gold
UK - Platinum
USA - Platinum x 10

THE ALBUMS & VIDEOS

If the **Hammer Time** collection captured him as a pop star for posterity, the Grammy award winning **Please Hammer Don't Hurt 'Em: The Movie**, took Hammer a few stages further. Hammer has never forgotten the importance of remembering one's roots and trying to put something back into the community. Above all it is a quasi-autobiographical film about how you can achieve anything if you put your mind to it. As he explains, "I wrote it myself based on the events and activities that happened in my life. The church scene has evolved from my being a member of the church."

As well as playing himself, Hammer also plays the real star of the show, the hippest pastor in town, Reverend Pressure, whose sermons come complete with a hip-hop choir and a DJ on either side of the pulpit. Wearing robes and a bouffant hairdo Hammer/

Pressure stands up and testifies with the righteous fervour of Martin Luther King infused with the charisma of Little Richard. Each sentence is punctuated by a bluesy run on the church organ built into his lectern. There's no stopping Pressure once he gets started. As he explains they call him Pressure because "I can take the heat." It's a triumphant 15 minute improvised set which is the celluloid centrepiece, showing that Hammer has an uncanny facility for humour, something that his critics rarely seem to notice. This pastor is a man possessed, but one triggered by Hammer's own teenage experiences in the local congregation where he first discovered the power of prayer. "When God brings you up, no man can bring you down." It's a sentiment which leads naturally into the clip for **Pray**, in which Hammer appropriates the hook from Prince's When Doves Cry, and the choir

assemble out in the park to contribute to one of the most rousing, inspirational moments of the movie.

The story is a simple one, corny even, but all the more powerful for its universal appeal. Hammer has made it big, and returns to Oakland to find that it has been overrun by drug barons who are using kids to help them deal dope. One day Hammer is with some children when they are caught in the crossfire of a gang war and one of them is killed. Hammer is furious and seeks out the criminals. When he finds them he makes them do the right thing, stop dealing and pay for a drug rehabilitation centre. He also makes them form DSAD - Drug Sellers Against Dope - and they have to put on a charity rap show to raise money. Of course Hammer gives his services free of charge for a storming show which provides the climax of the movie.

C-o-o-o-l M.C. Hammer T-shirts .... front .... and back.

It's a movie which puts other rappers in the shade, in pure entertainment terms, but it is also a movie with a moral. It acts as a reminder that Hammer will never forget where he came from. However big he becomes, his roots will always be there in Oakland. And therein resides one of the reasons why he has surpassed his rivals. Hammer's secret is to learn from the past, whether that's from Reverend Pressure, God, James Brown or Martin Luther King. As long as you don't forget about the past you will be able to make the future a better place. There's a sense of conviction that he puts into everything he does, from his albums and videos, to most importantly of all, the live shows. It's this amazing passion that makes the shows so memorable, intense and so spectacular. Once you have witnessed M.C. Hammer in action you would have to have a triple dose of amnesia to ever stand a chance of forgetting it.

Sights and sounds.

Let's Get It Started

The formalities over with, the show can now really start to swing, but before the second number of the evening can commence Hammer has to size up the audience. This means asking the crowd on the left to let out a deafening scream, and asking the crowd on the right if they can top it. The result has the desired effect, whipping the entire audience into a state of frenzy.

Some nights it's the people on the left who make the most noise, sometimes it's the people on the right. Most nights though, it's a dead heat, because everyone is bawling their lungs out for the next number. Hammer accordingly obliges. There's a thunderous drum roll from Tyrone Duncan, and Hammer declares that it's really "time to get started." He leaps into the second

number, **Let's Get It Started**, the title track from his debut album. Only a handful of years ago, back in Oakland, he was selling copies of this record from the boot of his car. Did he ever imagine then that he would one day be selling out at the most famous venues around the world, and equalling Michael Jackson as the biggest selling black artist in history?

Bust It Records artist Joey B. Ellis, who opened for Hammer in Japan and Europe.

"I can't hear you," Hammer tells his fans.

LET'S GET IT STARTED

On one side of the stage four little hammers bounce up and down in time with the music, which takes off at a frenzied pace. On the other, some graffiti is emblazoned in bright orange shades which reads, "Oakland Is Proud." It seems to sum up the mutual appreciation that flies between Hammer and his hometown. For this reason his Bust It Records operation is based there, while he makes his name known all around the globe.

With the audience hanging on his every word, Hammer's confidence bursts through as he struts to the front trading lines with his hype man Frosty. Frosty haunts Hammer across the stage like his shadow. Despite being the smaller of the duo, it's Hammer who steals the limelight, stalking around and pumping out his torso during the chorus, in between firing his groin out at the audience. It's an act which is both bullish and funny, part peacock and part parody of all those aggressive rappers that Hammer has transcended in the popularity stakes by being Mr Nice Guy.

It's typical of the way Hammer's operation has an air of democracy, that Frosty is out there tonight. This time last year Frosty was just plain Brian Sneed, one of Hammer's touring administrative team. During the world tour Hammer decided to use some different performers up front with him. Dancer QZ did the business on the antipodean leg, but for the European part of the tour Hammer suggested Sneed. Before you could say "Hammertime," Sneed laid down his mobile-phone, put on some shoulder-padding and become the supercool Frosty, performing in front of crowds of over ten thousand fans every night.

Hammer has some stiff competition from his dancers who are warming up as well now. The women who earlier in the day were giggling girls in casual trainers, grey sweat pants and T-shirts are nowhere to be seen. Instead Hammer's posse have done a Superman-in-a-phone-booth routine and become Amazon women in dayglo lycra, cutting a stylish swathe through the stage as Hammer moonwalks out at the front. Sometimes it seems as if there are about twenty five stars out there all battling for pole position. In the interests of fair play let's call it a draw.

Band & Singers

Hammer's band have only been together since he toured America in 1990, but to hear them play you'd think he had been working with them for his entire lifetime. These are experienced musicians and singers, which shows through every key change and gear shift of pace. This is a band who can crank it up for tracks such as **Pray** and **U Can't Touch This**, and then in mid flight bring it right down again for **Help The Children** and **Have You Seen Her**. The rhythmic backbone is provided by drummer Tyrone Duncan.

There's a rock and roll cliché that drummers are traditionally dumb, but don't try that one on Duncan. Known to his friends as Super, he's a complete natural. In fact it turns out that - though it is hard to believe - he has never had a lesson in his thirty two years on the planet. He just picks up a beat and runs with it, something which is easy for a man who first picked up a pair of drumsticks at the age of five. Along with bassist Kenny Franklyn, Tyrone makes the set go with a swing, revealing his strong leanings towards easy jazz and bands like Tower of Power

Hammer hand-picked his musicians with a keenness for both instinct and experience. The same mix comes from the brass section - Horns Of Fire. Ray Brown on trumpet, Gary Bias on saxophone and Reggie Young on trombone, are no slouches. They started out with Hammer on some TV shows early this year and stayed on. They usually play with funk veterans Earth, Wind and Fire. While that group is off the road, Ray Brown is more than happy with Hammer, but it's very different from his usual band. "It's unusual because Hammer is a rap artist. But then again there is a hell of a lot more to him than to most rap artists." Now fully ensconced as part of the famous Hammer team, the Horns will be appearing on his next album. Brown, who is doing the horn arrangements, has great hopes for the new LP, one which should see their employer moving further away from his rap roots and into the soul mainstream. "Hammer's new album is gonna have a lot more music on it, much more than most rap artists."

But it isn't just the musicians who are integral cogs in the Hammer sound. One of the most dynamic elements of the show are vocal group The Real Seduction, four men in sharp suits and even sharper haircuts. Like an old style James Brown revue, Tracy and Stacy Branden, Dennis and Sir Lawrence Pearce are part of the main attraction, but they are also an act in their own right. Chatting to them backstage, the identical twins, Stacy and Tracy, alias Double Trouble, fill in their background. Lively and likable, they constantly break into song mid-sentence, conversing in rhythm, "We've been together ten years. We got together back in New

The Horns of Fire: Reggie Young, Ray Brown and Gary Bias with Charles Freeman the merchandising co-ordinator.

The Real Seduction (from top clockwise): Sir Laurence Pierce, Stacy Branden, Dennis Gorden and Tracy Branden.

BAND & SINGERS

Sir Laurence Pierce warming up his vocal cords.

M.C. Hammer and QZ onstage.

Orleans in high school." Like many of the dancers, they started out performing on street corners, but they were swiftly picked up by Levi's and used in their ads. Since then their close harmonies have been used to sell everything from Pepsi to McDonalds.

Their style is rooted in America's traditional '50s close harmony doowop groups. They prefer to call themselves 'New-wop,' because, as Stacy explains, "It's drawn from the '50s and '60s,

bands like the Temptations and Four Tops, but we've put some modern character into it, giving it an upbeat '90s kind of feel."

It's a sound that they've lent to more superstars than they can remember. Over the years they've sung on albums by everyone from Terence Trent D'Arby to Natalie Cole, Pieces Of A Dream to Labella, Was Not Was to Club Nouveau, Pebbles to The Neville Brothers and perhaps inevitably, James Brown. But no tour to date

has been as much fun as Hammer's. It's given them a chance to show off, do some fancy footwork, and most of all take their New-wop around the world. As Stacy says, "We really appreciate Hammer giving us the chance to join him onstage." At the same time as being part of Hammer's posse, they've been able to maintain their own, unique identity. "Because remember..." as they say in perfect spontaneous harmony, "...We are the Reeeeeal Seduction."

BAND & SINGERS

U CAN'T TOUCH THIS !

BAND & SINGERS

Hammer's producer, musical director and keyboard player Felton Pilate consults with a technician.

Help The Children

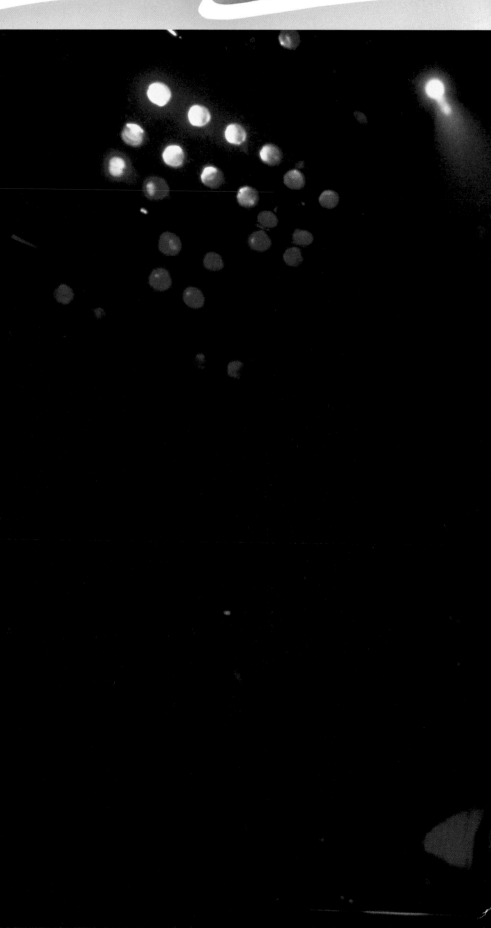

With the controls turned onto full steam ahead from the very start of the show, it's no surprise that Hammer has to slow the pace down every now and again. Despite a phenomenal display of stamina proving without a doubt that Hammer is more than just fit, even superstars have to catch their breath. As the dancers leave the stage after **Let's Get It Started** you can literally see the steam rising from their backs.

Hammer stays onstage though, and with his usual generosity-takes the opportunity to introduce his backing singers The Real Seduction, "the ladies choice." The ladies choice now come down off their perch at the back and do their stuff at the front of the stage, smiling and trucking along gently. Hammer does them proud with his introductions and potted biographies, which emphasise their romantic prowess - Sir Lawrence, for instance, "is hard to contain."

Not to be outdone by these latter-day Lotharios, Hammer has by now stripped down to the waist, a pair of taut braces holding his trousers in place. Hammer's perfect, rippling torso glistens under the lights as he glides across the floor, the Gene Kelly influence showing through in every soft-shoe shuffle. Eventually though, the emphasis shifts away from the singers to the audience. Hammer freezes as the music stops and fixes his eyes on the auditorium. As if moved by what he sees, he pauses, prowls around and delivers a plea for peace around the world, for

U CAN'T TOUCH THIS !

HELP THE CHILDREN

everyone, "We're concerned for all the children, the boys, girls, brothers, sisters, nieces and nephews, who, if we're not careful, may not live to see tomorrow."

When Hammer was starting out he always said that he wanted to rap in a different way, "I wanted to do rap with a positive message." This heartfelt sentiment leads him logically into **Help The Children**, Hammer's most humanitarian homily that borrows liberally from Marvin Gaye's equally passionate hymn to universal understanding, Mercy, Mercy, Me. During the song Hammer doesn't so much sing, as speak the lines, pulling out a large white hanky to mop away a combination of sweat and tears. On the giant video screens on either side of the stage, the young faces of the audience merge together as one as they sway in unison, arms aloft and eyes glazed over, hypnotised by the beat.

It's a song which for Hammer pulls together all sorts of strands of black music's history. Not only is that great soul advocate Marvin Gaye in there, but the song also conjures up other images from the black hall of fame, Nelson Mandela and Martin Luther King, figures that have been a spiritual, political and an intellectual influence on Hammer, both as a boy in Oakland, and today as a superstar. His performance might be pure showbiz, but Hammer would not be here today if these great icons had not given him the strength to pursue his goals. It may be schmaltzy, but that

doesn't mean it isn't sincere. As if his sincerity needed proving, Hammer has been responsible for setting up the Help The Children Foundation, into which he has channelled a great deal of his own money. Its aim is to help young, under-privileged kids in America find good jobs, to study hard at college and, most importantly of all, to avoid lapsing into crime, the fate that M.C. Hammer so very nearly succumbed to himself.

Hammer obliges a young fan with a smile and an autograph.

HELP THE CHILDREN

Hammer launches the Japanese tour, sponsored by Toshiba and Pepsi, in Tokyo ....

.... and entertains some Toshiba executives ....

.... while the Japanese press clamour for pictures.

Barnet Sneed & Vincent Rones (production assistants), T.C., Hammer, Craig Brooks and "Diamond" Ken.

Hammer by SydneyHarbour bridge, Australia.

The Posse

Hammer always knew that when the time came to take his show on the road he would have to do something different from his contemporaries. Something that would put him up there with Michael Jackson and Madonna as an all-round entertainer. It was a situation he was actually aware of when he prepared for a world tour to start in March 1991. "Last year M.C. Hammer was at one point. I could have been satisfied making another album which sounded just like the last one, like a lot of artists do, and going for record sales again, but that wouldn't be M.C. Hammer the person. I want to go to another level, expand, come out on tour with a live band, twenty five people on stage at the same time, and give you songs with saxophones, trumpets, the works..." Most of all 'the works' meant dancers. Hammer had always had a small posse with him from his early days rapping to playbacks around the clubs of Oakland's East Bay area, but this was something else. During 1990 on his American tour he travelled around checking out dance crews to find the best in the business. What he ended up with went far beyond anybody's wildest dreams - this is a dancing machine that would have given Fred Astaire a run for his money.

One of the most distinctive hoofers in the posse is Richard Whitebear, better known as Swoop. Twenty one years old, he is instantly recognisable because of his home-made range of hats that he keeps on around the clock. "I don't let anyone know

THE POSSE

Left to right: Three of the dancers. Shelby, No Bones and Goofy.

what I have under my hat, that's my style." At times onstage you suspect they are superglued to his head, otherwise they'd come off as he twirls and flips across the stage. As he ducks and dives across the floor you can see how he acquired his highly appropriate nickname.

Swoop started working with Hammer around Christmas when, as he explains, he was discovered. "I'm from Kansas City, Missouri. Before Hammer, I was in a drill team called the Marching Cobras, dancing and stepping to drums with my cousin No Bones, in tuxedos and stuff.

We always did different steps, making them up. We were the bold ones, we'd try to do anything to be original. We wanted to challenge Hammer, that's how we got to be with him. At the same time I was in a dance crew called the Imperial Preps with No Bones and Goofy, and we

The Posse in pants.

were doing a gig. Hammer came along and afterwards his masseur told us to come to the hotel. We auditioned for Hammer and he liked us, but two weeks later he asked us to come and audition again onstage with him. It was a real gig, a real baptism of fire, so we couldn't mess up."

Not only does Hammer write the music and perform, he is also the posse's choreographer. But, as Swoop elaborates, there is enough flexibility within the structure to allow the posse to do their own thing. "Everyone works together on the moves, I like to do solos, then Hammer comes in, checks it out, and adds in what he wants. He likes to work with the group in the studio."

If there's one thing the dancers have in common, it is that none

of them have had any professional training. It's hard to believe when you see them in action, but most of them picked their steps up off the streets. "We learnt jazz and tap by using our eyes and from watching TV. We've never been to school, that's why we mix styles into routines. But we do our own things on top, like doing tap moves but without tap shoes." It's this unconventional approach and irreverence for dance tradition that makes them stand out, but according to Swoop, it has also resulted in some accidents. "Most of our injuries have been because we've performed on different types of stages, and we like to wear patent leather shoes with rubber soles which aren't always right. Most of the time somebody has their knees and ankles wrapped up to avoid breaking them. I've

Cruising in Australia.

Weapons with Randall Gilbert, alias Randy Gee. A ball of energy bouncing around the bus as it travels to the gigs, QZ recounts how he came to be part of Hammer's crew, "I used to have red hair back then, and about two years ago I came to Hammer to audition for his movie, and I've been with him ever since." Travelling around the world, one of the best things is that there are so many performers together. It's more than just a band, it's like the movie Fame come to life. "It's like school, we hang close together and have a good time, just relax."

By comparison QZ's spar, Randy Gee, is more laid back, as if weighed down by the heavy gold necklace with his name on, hanging around his neck. Randy used to work in a bank, and officially he is still at college studying business. He went to them and got permission to take a year off so that he could tour with Hammer. "I'm twenty three now, but I figure I

just got back after a back problem. I have a thick spine but a small bone, so it's delicate. Some people have fallen off the stage, but you've gotta work on your balance."

A great admirer of Hammer, Swoop has similar ambitions. "I'm working on my singing. I'm not always gonna be dancing behind a rapper, I plan on being like Fred Astaire, Sammy Davis Junior and Gregory Hines."

Some of the other dancers have been associated with Hammer for some time now. Larry Rodgers, know as QZ, is the youngest member of the troupe at nineteen, but before he worked with Hammer he was in Oaktown's 3.5.7, who were the support group on Hammer's last tour. Originally from St Louis, Missouri, and a dancer since he was five, QZ started out in an Oakland group called the Lethal

can dance for a few more years yet. I've been lucky, I haven't had any serious injuries. But when I stop I'd like to stay involved, maybe go into management."

The women in the posse tend to be a little younger than the guys, and in contrast to their brash, confident, man-eating appearance onstage, they take their work very seriously, and are a little more bashful whilst travelling to and from gigs. Some

honed their acts on TV's Soul Train show, but like the men, most of them learnt their freestyle steps on the street. While the men rap along to the music coming out of the speakers, the girls prefer to sit quietly looking at the view as the bus travels around from gig to gig.

The most amazing thing is that the dancers are so fit. Their make-up isn't the only thing that runs throughout the show. There

is no special secret about keeping fit. M.C. Hammer works out and does three hundred sit-ups a day, but the dancers seem able to keep in shape just by going on stage and doing their routines in front of a live audience. Despite their media-made reputation for monastic devotion to duty, they seem to lead fairly regular lives. According to Uvanda, "My dancing keeps me fit. When you are in shape and on tour you build up stamina. I don't work out

The posse head towards the stage .... relax !

THE POSSE

U CAN'T TOUCH THIS !

Hammer - stage right !

with weights, I eat pretty much anything that I want." Swoop confesses to similar dietary indiscretions. "We are told what we should eat, but we always hit McDonalds and Burger King."

While most of the posse come from the American West Coast, the most distinctive of the female dancers - Yo-Yo - was discovered in her native Hawaii. "Hammer saw me in a club competition. He stood there watching me for 10 minutes, and then said 'come along with me.' I thought he was joking, but the next day I packed my bags and flew to Florida. That was over a year and a half ago, and I've been with him ever

since." Like the rest of the posse Yo-Yo hasn't had any professional training, but she ended up training others. "I'd been a street dancer learning from the kids in my neighbourhood, and then I became an instructor teaching them to get into dancing and stay off drugs. But at the same time I used to enter dance contests and win - probably because I was the only female dancer."

But of all the movers and shakers, the one that literally stands out in any crowd is No Bones. Called No Bones because, as anyone who has seen him turning into a human four-legged spider in the show will know, he is double-

jointed. He's easy to spot as the band loiter in the foyer waiting for the bus to take them to the gig, because his hair stands head and shoulders above everybody. From some angles it looks like he has a cobra on his head, from others it looks like a giant walnut whip. Whatever way you look at it, the question you have to ask is 'how does he get it like that?' and more importantly, 'how does he keep it like that throughout the 105 minute show?' The answer it transpires, is fiendishly simple. "It's amazing that people always ask me that. I just use lots of gel and hairspray. But the real trick is to hold my head down while it dries!"

The band always makes a colourful impact on arrival at a hotel.

NO BONES - but a <u>lot</u> of hairspray.

Hammer always 'makes it smooth'.

Pray

Before the next number, M.C. Hammer pauses for a dedication. "We're sending this out to all the young men and women who fought for peace in the Gulf. And we wanna send this one out to all of you who believe prayer can help to keep the peace, because we know we've got to pray just to make it today."

The stage has been bare for a while now, but in an instant it is besieged by bodies. Costumes have been changed, and the skimpy skin-tight outfits are gone. In their place are purple and black cassocks. As the posse sway from side to side, Busby Berkeley meets the Archbishop of Canterbury. **Pray** is the part of the show which most closely resembles the video. Hammer, out front, alternates from conducting his funky choir - recalling his Reverend Pressure character from his videos - and addressing the audience, his very own congregation. Hammer must be one of the few preachers with three razor sharp tram lines cut into his hair, and a Ferrari Testarossa parked in his garage.

But **Pray** is no ordinary gospel chant, one of Hammer's funkiest hits, it draws on Prince's When Doves Cry for its melodic backbone. What Hammer has done is totally reshape the song, turning a self-centred melodrama into a interdenominational, hummable hymn with the slickest groove in town. It's not just the posse that are up on its feet, the audience are clamouring for more, being geed up by the dancers as they clap along and wave their hands in the air.

By the time the song reaches its crescendo, the audience is at fever pitch. But Hammer pushes them off rap's Richter scale when he teases them and bellows, "Somebody make some noise." This is followed by some rudimentary rhetoric enquiries, "Are there any ladies in the house? Are there any fellas in the house?" The answer is a very loud and categorical yes.

Suddenly "Everybody dance now" comes out of the loudspeakers. Everybody does precisely that, building up for one of the high spots of the show's dance routines. On the stage things become competitive as each member of the posse goes to the centre to do their own thing. Each dancer outdoes the last, if one spins on his bottom, the next spins on his back. If one does a backflip, the next does two backflips. It is almost as exhausting to watch as it is to do. The mesmerising thing is that everyone does something different - it's a real chance for the team to do some freestyle showing off. As if it was ever in doubt, they've proved they can dance. But Hammer wants to know something else, "Can they pump it up?"

On the surface this is a pretty simple exercise, involving much billowing out of harem pants and pushing one's pelvis out into the audience. Hammer has been off the stage for a while, and now back, he makes his presence felt by driving his groin into a frenzy, as a rat-tat-tat, machine gun, drum roll provides the percussive accompaniment.

But this only makes the rest of the posse try harder. First up is Randy Gee on the right of the stage. It isn't just his groin that bounces into action, but his whole body, as he wobbles, ripples and spins around like an uncoiling spring. Not bad, muses Hammer. But QZ on the left can do better. Firstly he stretches his trouser belt out to check that everything is in order inside. Then away he goes, shuffling, shimmying and oscillating in orgasmic spasms across the stage as if electrified. It's not surprising that at the end of it he wiggles and passes out. Then it's No Bones' turn. The man with the rubber physique pumps it up Spiderman-style, folding himself into a ball and suspending himself on his hands as he rocks up and down. Beat that!

The Real Seduction can't really compete in the raw, unbridled male sexuality stakes. Or can they? Their way of pumping it up is smooth but deadly. Cruising to the front of the stage, they croon a while, and then, just as you think they don't have it in them, bang, bang, bang, bang. They can pump it up with the rest of them.

But anything the men can do, the women can do too. The ladies of Soft Touch line up smiling and smirking. Each has a man at her hips invigilating. They certainly get a shock when the women go into action, the force of their pumping knocking the judges flying. Most of them get up, but No Bones is out for the count, and his limp, jelly-like frame has to be stretchered off by the rest of the posse.

PRAY

The climax of the routine though is Yo-Yo, the dancer who pumps it up Hawaiian style. Everyone is silent except for the gasps and sighs of the men, and the rhythm section which grooves along as she slithers across the stage, rising and falling like a snake in time with the beat. It's not surprising to find out that during the tour she strained her back and had to take time off to recuperate. Most of the dancers could win medals in Olympic gymnastics, but Yo-Yo would bag golds for a lifetime.

MC HAMMER

Backstage

The most important area backstage is the food area. For the world's fittest road-show there has got to be input for there to be output, so food is of the essence. On one trip across Europe the band had to stop for so many meals that a journey that should have taken only about 16 hours, took well in excess of 33 instead.

But to keep lean and in good physical shape Hammer steers clear of excess. During the day he doesn't eat much more than some fruit, and drinks plenty of Pepsi and fresh orange juice. Hammer's appetite switches on when he comes off stage. Each night Royston, the chef, prepares a special meal for him of chicken cooked with fresh mangoes and

spices. Coming back to earth after his mentally and physically draining performance, Hammer likes to eat in the privacy of his own dressing room. The rest of his band and crew all eat together in one of the specially constructed restaurants. These are very different to the West Coast clubs Hammer's posse grew up around, but they soon

M.C. Hammer and Brian Harris, EMI record executive, in Australia.

Hammer grabbing a chance to relax with a quick game of basketball.

BACKSTAGE

M.C. Hammer with his brother and personal manager Louis Burrell.

M.C. Hammer with his ever vigilant production manager Jeff Mason.

BACKSTAGE

M.C. Hammer in Oz.

Rehearsing for the 1991 American Music Awards.

make themselves at home, thanks to showbusiness caterers Eat Your Heart Out, led by the diligent, efficient and frighteningly energetic Linda.

The biggest group in the music world deserves the biggest caterers. Eat Your Heart Out's last job was travelling around the world with Paul McCartney. The eight person team have been travelling with Hammer on their own crew bus since the first European date on April 9th in Rotterdam. It's a hard life on the road for the cooks, which requires a lot of dedication as they have to be the first ones at the venue so that they can prepare breakfast for the riggers and production people. Usually they get in at 8am, and they don't leave much before 1am. In between they feed about one hundred and fifty people on delicacies like jerk pork chops and oat-breaded halibut. They use up to about sixty eight kilograms of potatoes and thirty fresh French sticks, as well as enough soft drinks and juices to float a liner.

BACKSTAGE

Tonight for the vegetarians there's cheddar and garlic ravioli. There are about twenty vegetarians, and one of them is Mike Gambrell, the masseur for Hammer and the posse. Gambrell, who speaks in a bass growl that seems to come from his navel, has been with Hammer throughout his career. He helps him to tone up his body and keep all the toxins out of his system so that he can perform at his peak each night. Gambrell is not just a masseur, but the ship's doctor, tending to any ailments that crop up. Rather than use drugs, he prefers 'natural medicine and vitamins.' His magic hands help, but the real secret of good health, Gambrell confides, is "Physical and mental fitness." If that's the case, Hammer's team shouldn't have a sick day in their lives

Tom Jones surrounded by Hammer's posse.

BACKSTAGE

M.C. Hammer in his Lincoln Continental 'convertible' !

Round by the VIP lounge, some children from a local school have been lucky enough to win the chance to meet Hammer. Tense beforehand, afterwards they are all squeals and blushes, recalling how Hammer put his arm around them. "It's made my day." says one. "It's made my year." says another. A third trumps the other two with, "It's made my life!"

The youngsters then get an added bonus of the band arriving. They certainly know how to make an entrance, strutting in with boom-boxes on their shoulders and canes at their sides. There are suits of all shades, and enough lurex to redecorate a thousand discos. And this is just the men. By comparison the women are more subtle, mostly dressed down in sweat-pants and T-shirts, saving their extravagant side for 'showtime' when they are trans-formed into ultra-aggressive Amazons. The organised panic

Hammer with his brother Louis and his long time friend and tour manager Craig Brooks.

that ensues before each show is about to be transformed into the zen-like thrill of 'showtime.'

Just before the gig the atmosphere is one of subdued activity. No-one sees much of Hammer, who shuts himself away to pump some iron and limber up. Back at the rest of the group's dressing rooms, each component of the show is doing their own thing. The Real Seduction are breaking into song, the brass section, the Horns Of Fire, are practising, and some of the dancers are warming up so that they don't go on cold and strain a muscle. Some do a spot of shadow boxing, others mess around giving each other piggy back rides. Swoop and No

Bones have their own unique way of warming up. They stretch their legs by shinning up the underbelly of the raised auditorium beneath the growing crowd. Shouting and joking at the audience through the gaps in the scaffolding they don't seem to have a care in the world.

Worries are left to production manager Jeff Mason, who looks after everything from checking that the keyboards are plugged in, to making sure that the gates are open to admit Hammer's Lincoln Continental. Mason, who has been with Hammer through the States, New Zealand, Australia, Japan and now Europe, is the most unlikely production manager you are ever liable to meet. Bearded, bespectacled and dressed in a tweed jacket with leather armpatches, he looks more like your friendly neighbourhood physics teacher than one of the most experienced fixers in the business. He has worked with everyone from Queen to Rod Stewart to Prince to Earth Wind And Fire, and back again. Mason's only affectation is to suck in a cigarette held in a long black ivory holder. Jeff Mason's inner sanctum is the nerve centre of the live operation. Locked tightly away like Fort Knox are the special backstage passes with Hammer's distinctive logo on them, in the corner there's the obligatory portable fax, a pile of mobile-phones, and on the wall three clocks. A red one which gives LA time, a white one with European time and a yellow one with correct UK time, which says underneath, "The centre of the universe."

M.C. Hammer pre-show in Tokyo.

Cab Calloway

Raphael Wiggins & Tim Christian
(members of Tony! Toni! Tone!)

Louis & Stevie Wonder

Hakeem Abdulsamad of The Boys

Khiry Abdulsamad of The Boys

Louis & Woopie Goldberg

Have You Seen Her

Of all of Hammer's rap remakes, **Have You Seen Her** is the one which stays the most faithful to the original version. First recorded by vocal group The Chi-Lites back in the early '70s, Hammer has adapted the words to bare his soul and tell a very personal story of his own lost love.

Once again the stage is cleared of dancers as Hammer recalls how he can't get his girlfriend out of his mind since he found her in the arms of another man. The Real Seduction provide an ethereal refrain which runs through the spine of the song as Hammer sings about his broken heart. He reveals to Frosty how it is difficult to cry because he is a man. Frosty consoles him with the modern advice that there is no shame in a man crying. In fact Hammer should go ahead and let his emotions out instead of bottling them up. The whole scene is acted out as a sentimental tearjerker, while Hammer comes to terms with his romantic grief and sobs on cue.

The mawkish moments don't last too long as **Have You Seen Her** segues into a solo dance routine. Until now Hammer's moves have had to take place alongside his posse. Here he is alone as he evolves, or rather revolves, into a human turntable. Spinning on a coin, Hammer mimics the scratched disc sounds coming from his DJs at the back, twirling on the spot like a stylus, backwards and forwards in time with the beat. Up on the video screens the technicians have worked a great piece of magic, merging Hammer's figure with a record deck so that he looks like he is playing the music with his body. Waving his hanky in the air, Hammer runs through some of his sharpest moves, cutting a dashing figure in his trademark 'Leaning Tower' pose.

This solo brings the house down, but doesn't seem to have pleased Frosty who struts back on to tell Hammer that he and the posse are unhappy. Frosty says the audience doesn't know how to party. Hammer disagrees, "We've been partying all night." But it's to no avail, Frosty and the posse are unhappy and have decided to leave. There's a moment of genuine anxiety as the audience wonders whether this onstage confrontation is unrehearsed and for real. Then the theme from the classic American cop series Dragnet plays, and it becomes apparent that this is another routine. No one knows the outcome. Even Turbo B from support band Snap stands on the stage arguing with Hammer. Insults are traded but Hammer doesn't seem to want to apologise to Frosty. If he wants to go that's fine, and if he wants to take the posse with him, well that's fine too. Hammer has a trick up his sleeve, and the audience is on his side. He gestures to Frosty to leave as the crowd bellows in one voice, "See ya" which almost blows the muscular vocalist off his patent leather shoes. Hammer's not worried, "I'm gonna get me a new posse, And I'm gonna get it from right here." Hammer may have been deserted, but in the best traditions of the Broadway musical, the show must go on...

Fans

Hammer would never have made it without his fans. From his earliest days selling records from the boot of his car in Oakland, to girdling the globe on the current tour, Hammer has been cementing his relationship with his audience. As he constantly reiterates during the concert, without the children there would be no future for the world. There would also be no M.C. Hammer phenomenon. It's remembering facts like this that keeps Hammer humble and makes him constantly aware of who put him where he is today.

At whichever grand hotel the band are based, there is always a gaggle of giggling fans holding an almost constant vigil. They sit on a nearby wall outside, swapping stories about Hammer - who has seen him the most, who has got the most autographs. Every now and again their patience is rewarded when M.C. Hammer emerges through the entrance and gets into his Lincoln Continental to go and do some shopping.

Other members of Hammer's entourage also poke their heads out to meet and greet the fans. Dancer Swoop is one of the early risers, and when he isn't watching Dick Tracy on video, he likes to hang out with the kids who aren't much younger than him. The youngest member of the posse, QZ, also pops outside the sanctuary of the hotel every now and again to shoot the breeze and swap gum with the local home-boys.

As 5pm approaches on show days, the crowd grows to wish the band bon voyage as they head to the gig in their two coaches. The original pop picket line begins to disperse around now, making their own way to the gig to try and beat the band.

By 7pm the front rows are awash with the faithful. Most are women and girls, but there is always a healthy smattering of boys who admire and display 100% commitment to Hammer. Despite the security guards' best efforts to keep them in their seats, they squeeze to the front barrier to try

A young fan on stage holds M.C. Hammer's hand for comfort.

FANS

to catch a glimpse of the crew backstage. Every time a black face appears, one of the girls screams "It's Hammertime." It isn't yet, but the waiting is all part of the fun.

In trying to analyse the M.C. Hammer success story by far the best people to ask are the ones who have made him such a huge success. Shauna, who is eighteen and nearly breathless with anticipation, has given considerable thought to the subject. "You can tell with M.C. Hammer that he means what he says. Other pop groups and rappers like Vanilla Ice just boast about themselves. Hammer talks about real life and real people. That's why everyone likes him, even my mum and dad like him!" Michelle strongly believes that Hammer cares far more than most other rappers and doesn't have any pretensions, "Hammer looks after his dancers, he doesn't let them out at night. He doesn't make a secret out of the fact that he comes from the street."

Europe might be a long way from the streets of Oakland, but Hammer inspires the same kind of loyalty from his fans here as he does at home. Jill, whose bedroom wall currently boasts about a hundred, and rising, different pictures of Hammer, pays special attention to what he sings about. "M.C. Hammer is very dedicated. We'll follow him and do whatever he says. We take in everything. We might not think about it at the time, but later on we will, and if he says 'don't take drugs' or something, we listen to that."

Some of the crowd have come an extremely long way to see the show. Shauna bought her ticket back in January on the day the tour was announced, and has travelled over 700 miles to experience and see M.C. Hammer.

It's **Hammertime** !

There's no doubting their commitment to their hero - you get the impression that even if there had been a train strike, seventeen year old Jill would have walked the 200 miles from her hometown just to be there tonight.

But away from Hammer's views it's his performance that really sends his fans into a frenzy. Shauna thinks he's even better onstage than in his videos. "He's the only one in the entire universe who knows how to dance. M.C. Hammer's movements are his, and he perfected them. Then he gave them to everybody else. It's like his music - he might have used old records, but he updates them and makes them better. He's better than Michael Jackson and Bobby Brown." It's not just his music that Shauna admires though, "His music is great dance music, but his body is an important part of it too. If he had no muscles we'd say 'You skinny bastard, get off the stage.' We've all tried to copy his dance moves, but no-one can imitate him. He's the best!"

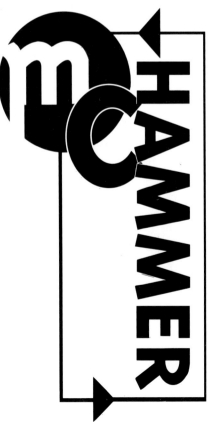

U Can't Touch This

With Frosty having taken Hammer's posse away with him, the fans are wondering how he is going to recruit a new posse at such short notice. What they have been unaware of is that during the set Hammer's security team have been wandering through the auditorium looking for the best dancers. During **Have You Seen Her** a dozen were selected and taken backstage where they've been waiting for their moment of stardom. Right on cue they mount the steps and each night become the unlikeliest members of Hammer's new posse.

The boys haven't got the muscles of the old posse, and the girls haven't got the figures, in fact most of them are under ten years old. But no problem, Hammer auditions them anyway one by one. Little kids in junior Reeboks and sweat pants split and slide and hip hop across the stage like mini M.C.s, and one by one are greeted with Hammer's endorsement, "She's in the posse, he's in the posse." Of course it doesn't always work out. On one night, one of the children had an attack of stage fright - understandable really in front of a crowd of thirteen thousand - and was frozen to the spot. But Hammer's the generous type - he got in the posse anyway.

There are also some special invitations handed out for some VIPs - very important posses. On one night actor James Belushi got up onstage and passed the posse test. And on the final night in London there were some very special kids seconded into the

"Do you want to be in the posse?" asks Hammer.

U CAN'T TOUCH THIS

posse - the New Kids On The Block - who were due to start their own UK tour the following night. This stunt, concocted with all the best intentions, actually turned out to be one of the most embarrassing moments of the tour. As Hammer introduced his "special friends" the audience started booing in a show of playful rap rivalry. Backstage though you could see that, for a moment, Danny, Jordan and Joey hesitated as if they were having second thoughts about going on. It was a tribute to their good nature, and the fact that they liked Hammer so much, that they braved the boos and joined the posse onstage. With a new allstar posse bringing up the rear, Hammer's show is unassailable. As the man says himself, "You know **U Can't Touch This**."

At this, the beat of Hammer's biggest hit to date starts to kick, and the new posse springs to life. In fact the beat is so irresistible that the old posse soon returns for Hammer's greatest hit. The new power-charged version with added band swings like Cab Calloway, and then at the chorus Hammer gets everyone to wave their hands, creating a Mexican wave across the auditorium.

It's the show at its very peak. The stage is packed with dancers of all colours and styles, everyone is going mad. From the ceiling three enormous hammers come down and bounce up and down. As for the music, Hammer has upgraded Rick James' cult funk workout Superfreak, and turned it into an anthem for the '90s, embellished with brass, sweat and Hammer's heavenly rap. It is the song with which Hammer offers his public thanks to his biggest mentor of all. Not James Brown, not Cab Calloway, not Martin Luther King, but God. As Hammer declares, his music makes him say, "Oh my lord, thank you for blessing me with a mind of rhyme and two flash feet."

And then with a crack of the drums he's gone, but the audience are staying and have no intention of leaving for home yet. It's the night of their lives and they aren't about to let him get away so easily. A chant of "Hammer, Hammer, Hammer" goes up and sounds as if it won't ever stop. After 2 minutes Hammer comes back on. He's only got one thing to say. He probably knows the answer, but he asks it anyway. "Do you want more?"

U CAN'T TOUCH THIS

Clothes

During its evolution rap music has developed a very distinctive image. One with heavy gold necklaces dripping from necks, and the toughest leather trousers, that said much about the machismo and street-toughness of the genre. Hammer's clothes are equally distinctive, but the way they break free from the traditions of rap culture say much about the way Hammer's music has also broken away from the shackles that tie rap to the musical and literal black ghetto.

One of the first things to be delivered to every venue are the cases which hold the clothes for the show. Cases are perhaps understatements - these are more like small portable rooms. There are seven containers, each about 2 metres high and 1.5 metres wide, that look as if they could contain a couple of pianos each. In fact when they are opened they spill out a dazzling array of costumes in gold, red, pink and black, leather, silk and pretty much every colour and material under the sun. Sequins lurk everywhere, and there's one case simply bursting with matching white satin suits.

Hammer wears a little jewellery, but it is his costumes that do most of the glittering. They seem to come in all the hues of the rainbow, and all shapes and sizes, from circulation constricting lycra to his trademark silk baggies. His most distinctive look is the harem-style trousers that appeared around the time of the **U Can't Touch This** videos. Hammer has the final say in what

he wears, but his clothes designer Du Vual Parker has worked with him closely throughout his career, from the early days to his current tour. He is already working on some totally different and exciting ideas, which he is keeping under

his hat, for Hammer's next look, set to coincide with his new album.

Parker, who is descended from Red Indian stock, was born and raised in Oakland where he is at

M.C. Hammer watches Felton Pilate backstage in Tokyo.

the forefront of the company that owes much of its success to Hammer. "It's called Modertech - Modern Technology For The Mankind Of The Future, a whole new era in fashion design. My concept is to bring together high fashion and technology. The trouble with most fashion these days is that it goes around in a complete circle, always looking back to the past. I'm trying to take fashion further and up to another level. What I'm doing is making forward fashion clothing for forward fashion minded individuals, and M.C. Hammer is ideal because he is an open-minded individual. He expresses my personal creativity on the stage."

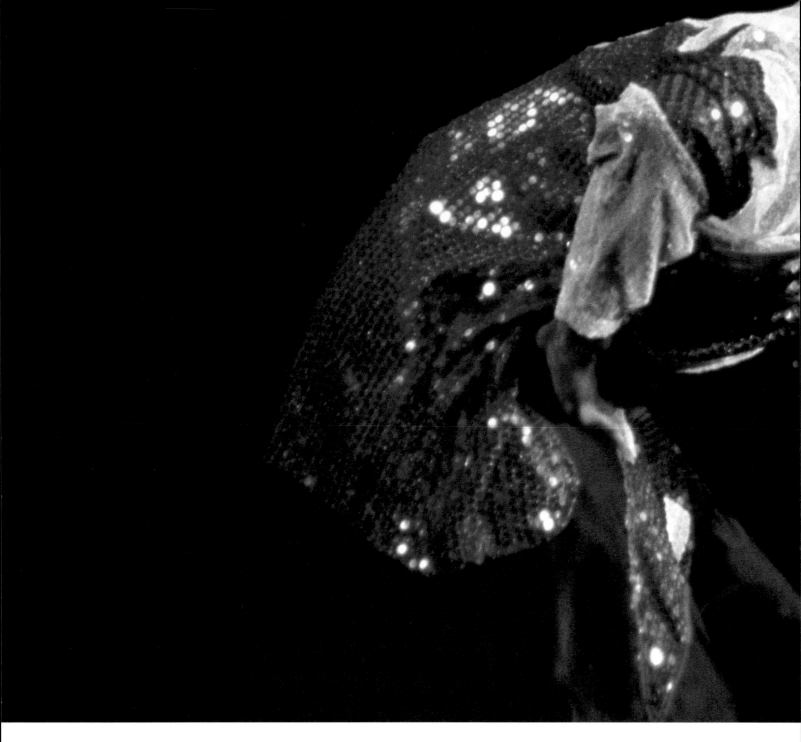

Just one of Hammer's many amazing outfits.

While Hammer was rehearsing for this tour, Parker was designing the stage costumes for everyone. But you'd be wrong to think his work finishes once the clothes are completed. His work is only just beginning. "Once we've made the costumes we have to maintain them." And it's a big job. Hammer alone has twenty seven different outfits, and the whole entourage has a staggering four thousand, seven hundred costumes. It's no surprise the operation takes on a marked similarity to painting a bridge. No sooner have Du Vual Parker and his team finished repairing the costumes from one set of tears and splits, than they are waiting to be repaired again. Not that this is any reflection on his craftsmanship, it's more to do with the stretches and contortions that the group undertake during each 105 minute performance. "Keeping them in good condition is not an easy task as you can imagine. And apart from the stitching there's the cleaning bills which come to $7000 a time."

In the future Parker predicts a move away from the baggy stuff into tighter outfits. You can already see the metamorphosis during the shows when Hammer tends to change in the middle into a simpler, more snug pair of black trousers. Parker also plans to use more spandex, the kind of material more normally sported by heavy metal guitarists. "It'll be a whole new concept for Hammer, above and beyond what we've done so far. We've gotta keep it private, but it's going to be an important fashion statement."

One of Derwin Parker's assistants is Jermaine from Louisiana. He also happens to be one of Hammer's cousins, keeping things a close-knit family affair. He first met Hammer when they were both 'real young,' but it was much later, in the summer of 1987, when Hammer was just getting started that they met again. At the time Hammer only had four dancers, but Jermaine could already see his potential. "I had an idea he would make it. There was something about him, he had style and determination."

One of the most striking members of Hammer's team of stylists is Mel Peters. While most of the crew sport short hair, Peters has shoulder-length, straightened black hair, making him stand out backstage almost as much as No Bones, the man with the pointy haircut. Mel has been doing everyone's make-up on the current tour, though Hammer and most of the men only wear make-up for video shoots. It takes about 2 hours to do everyone, but whereas at the beginning he had to do it all, now most of the

dancers are able to do it themselves, making his job a lot easier. "Everybody gets a little bit of something from me, but with the older girls I just need to check it." It's remarkable that somehow the pan-stick and gloss manages to keep in place throughout the show. Standing in the audience as they take their final bow, the faces still look immaculate, the eyes stand out and the lips are perfectly defined. But Peters lets out a playful titter and reveals a little secret, "You should see them up close."

Mel Peters puts the finishing touches to M.C. Hammer's hair.

Please Hammer Don't Hurt 'Em

Although there would be no show without Hammer, let us not forget the people who make things happen, in particular Louis Burrell, Craig Brooks and Felton Pilate. Louis K Burrell is Hammer's brother and personal manager. He is responsible for the day to day business affairs of the Hammer organisation. Louis also runs Bust It Records, the label he and Hammer own. Distributed by Capitol Records, Bust It artists include Joey B Ellis, B Angie B, Special Generation and Oaktown's 3.5.7. Craig Brooks is Hammer's tour manager. He's responsible for the touring party as they travel the world. Working with everyone from concert promoters to record label executives, Craig moves eighty five people in a smooth and efficient manner. He served in the Navy with Hammer, and they've been friends ever since. Felton Pilate is Hammer's producer and serves as musical director for the stage show. A founding member of the '70s funk band Con Funk Shun, Felton has been working with Hammer since the beginning. As musical director of the live show, he leads the band through its paces as they provide the musical setting for the posse's dance extravaganza.

When M.C. Hammer comes back on for his encore, what every member of the audience must think is "How can you top a magical pop extravaganza packed with so many memorable moments?" The answer is simple, you can't. But what you do get is a compressed version of everything that's gone before. He started by announcing his arrival with **Here Comes The Hammer**, and he finishes appropriately with the song which made his name a byword for the sensitive style of '90s rap, **Please Hammer Don't Hurt 'Em**.

It's as if the whole evening is passing before your eyes in an instant. The Cecil B De Millean excesses of the show all collide in the encore when the stage is filled with gyrating, aerobic bodies, grinding their way through the insistent, repetitive dancebeat. Some of the dancers are hyperactively freewheeling their way around the stage, others are running in strict formation up and down the sides. Still more are climbing up and down the platforms. The Real Seduction are leaning over the sides of their perch, encouraging the audience to sing along, while in between them still more dancers climb up, then leap down onto the main stage like funky lemmings. Even the keyboard players, Felton Pilate and Natalie Yco, are grooving to the throbbing beat behind their instruments. It's chaos, but rigidly regimented chaos, the team going into glitzy mega-drive and applauding the audience.

As the band slams into gear like an express train, the beat becomes more and more hypnotic. Hammer calls on the Horns Of Fire, and they respond mightily. Eventually though it has to wind down, as piece by piece instruments withdraw. Simultaneously the posse also withdraw from the stage, one by one retiring until drummer Tyrone propels his sticks into the crowd.

Eventually there's nothing left on the stage but the shirtless Hammer who is mopping his brow with a white towel, and a reverberating volcanic reggae bass beat. As punctually as it began, the clock reaches 11pm, and in a blaze of pyrotechnics three explosions suddenly erupt. The noise is deafening, the lights flash in time with the bangs and Hammer continues to dance at the front. The end is announced as Hammer tosses his sweat-stained towel into the audience. Some nights the towel is so heavily drenched it seems to fly halfway across the auditorium. Other nights it lands in the front rows, but wherever it lands it causes a mini-riot as those nearby, and some of those not so nearby, lunge for a rare memento of the show.

The audience refuses to leave. Many are still thumping their feet and stamping on their chairs, and the security team have to keep them away from the stage at the front. Many don't want to accept that it's over, but venue regulations prevent a second encore, and the house lights come up to bring the assembled blinking back to reality. Slowly and reluctantly they make their way to the exits, slightly hoarse of voice and sore of foot, but filled with the memories of having seen one of the most stunning live shows in pop history. Without a doubt the most fleshed out, fully realised and exquisitely syncopated performance by a rap artist in the history of the genre. This'll certainly take some beating. We'll probably have to wait until the next M.C. Hammer tour for that.

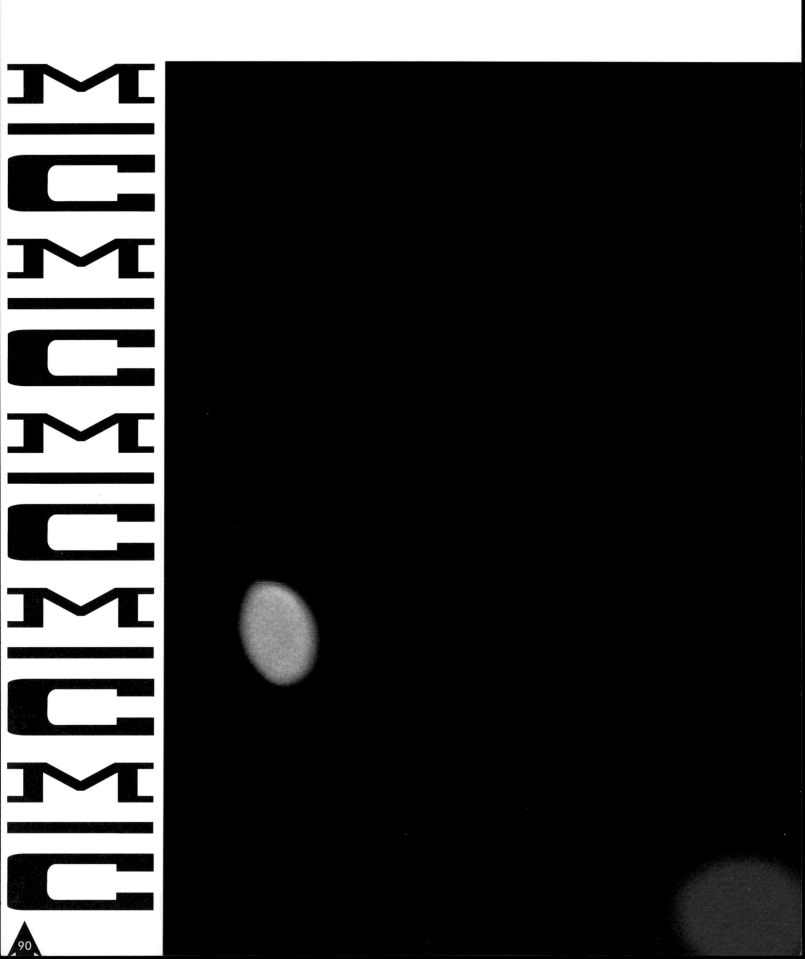

MC HAMMER

TOUR PERSONNEL

PERFORMERS

M.C. HAMMER

Gary Bias	Saxophone
Raymond Brown	Trumpet
Reginald Young	Trombone
Kenneth Franklyn	Bass Guitar
Michael Buckholtz	Keyboards
Felton Pilate	Keyboards
Natalie Yco	Keyboards
Angela Carter	Percussionist
Tyrone Duncan	Drummer
Joey B Ellis	Singer
Erica Bond	Background Singer
Stacy Branden	Background Singer
Tracy Branden	Background Singer
Carla Coleman	Background Singer
Benito Glosson	Background Singer
Dennis Gordon	Background Singer
Tynetta Hare	Background Singer
Trina Johnson	Background Singer
Laurence Pierce	Background Singer
Novella Simpson	Background Singer
Bryant Marable	D.J.
La Juanna Boykin	Dancer
Juanita Brown	Dancer
Rodney Butler	Dancer
Lisa Corpos	Dancer
Shelby Gates	Dancer
Randall Gilbert	Dancer
Uvanda Grady	Dancer
Tarhonda Harrison	Dancer
Yolanda Holck	Dancer
Michelle Jennings	Dancer
Larry Lamarr	Dancer
Renee Pettigrew	Dancer
Zester Ponder	Dancer
Larry Rodgers	Dancer
Junella Segura	Dancer
Jennifer Warren	Dancer
Richard Whitebear	Dancer
Niasha Wilson	Dancer
Shiralessia Worthen	Dancer
Russel Wright	Dancer

STAFF

Louis K Burrell	Personal Manager
Craig Brooks	Tour Manager
Clay Shell	Tour Accountant
Deryl Horton	Assistant Road Manager
Felton Pilate	Musical Director
Charles L Freeman	Merchandising Coordinator
Derwin Parker	Tailor
Calvin Hall	Wardrobe
Robin Horton	Wardrobe
Timothy Lewis	Valet
Joseph Mack	Valet
Michael Ishmael	Valet
Ronald Cooper	Valet
Lloyd Johnson	Valet
Jeffrey Houston	Hair Stylist
Kenneth Wright	Hair Stylist
Mel Peters	Make-up Artist
Mike Gambrell	Physical Therapist
George Livingstone	Photographer
Brad Harper	Pepsi Liason
Al Horton	Production Assistant
Darryl Horton	Production Assistant
Barnett Sheed	Production Assistant
Brian Sneed	Production Assistant
Kenneth Hunter	Production Assistant
Vincent Rones	Production Assistant
Barrie Marshall	Marshall Arts - Tour Promoter

TOUR PERSONNEL

CREW

Jeff Mason	Production Manager
Thomas Hudack	Stage Manager
Deborah Putnam	Production Assistant
Monica Maynard	Ambiance / Catering
Steven Jones	Assistant Stage Manager
Billy Evans	Venue Security
Robert McKenney	Rigger
Michael Singleton	PYRO Technician
Troy Hansen	Lighting Director
Gary Randel	Varilite Director
Robert Jarvis	#1 Very Handy Guy
Charles Cochran	#2 Very Handy Guy
Curtis Battles	Head Carpenter
Roger Cabot	Carpenter
Michael Tierney	Carpenter
Tim Colvard	House Engineer
Charles Klein	Monitor Engineer
Jaime Hurrieta	Sound Crew Chief
Harry Witz	Sound Consultant
William Kurts	Sound Crew
Arthur Dome	Sound Crew
Mark Dice	Video Director
Bruce Ramos	Video Crew Chief / Operator
Jana Sinclair	Camera Operator
Jay Strasser	Camera Operator
Gary Doon	Projectionist
Michael Pentz	Projectionist
John Jetty	Video Engineer
Robert Larson	Band Technician
Victor LeCromer	Band Technician
Nicola Burtan	Production Crew
Richard Peach	Production Crew
Jon Holt	Production Crew
Steve Rusling	Production Crew
Dave Morgan	Production Crew
Pete Russell	Production Crew
Martin Nicholas	Production Crew
Steven Yound	Production Crew
Ozzie Marsh	Production Crew
Thomas Hudale	Production Crew
Thomas Tierney	Production Crew
Andrew Becker	Catering Team
Metta Bergstrom	Catering Team
Catherine Duignan	Catering Team
Linda Gooding	Catering Team
Royston Lyons	Catering Team
John Quigley	Catering Team
Gillian Shapely	Catering Team
Jean-Claude Monard	Catering Team